The
Big
Bedtime
Book of
Bible Stories
and Prayers

The Big Bedtime Book of Bible Stories and Prayers

Debbie Trafton O'Neal

ILLUSTRATED BY JONATHAN SATCHELL

Abingdon Press
Nashville

The Big Bedtime Book of Bible Stories and Prayers
Copyright © 1995 *Hunt & Thorpe Ltd*
Text © 1995 *Debbie Trafton O'Neal*
Illustrations © 1995 *Jonathan Satchell*
Published in the United States of America by Abingdon Press
Designed by *The Bridgewater Book Company Ltd*

ISBN 0-687-00126-9

ABINGDON PRESS
PO Box 801, 201 Eighth Avenue South
Nashville, TN 37202-0801

The right of *Debbie Trafton O'Neal* and *Jonathan Satchell*
to be identified as author and illustrator of this work has been
asserted by them in accordance with the Copyright, Designs and
Patents Act 1988

A CIP catalogue record for this book is available
from the British Library

Printed and bound in Hong Kong

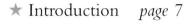

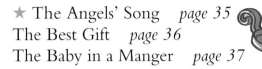

Contents

Introduction

For many families, bedtime is the perfect end to a perfect day. For others, bedtime is a time of frustration and chaos, but it doesn't have to be this way. Children do best when they have a regular routine and consistent time schedule for bedtime. Not only do their bodies adjust and react accordingly, they also begin to look forward to the time of rest that is such a necessary part of life. Of course, this varies according to the age of the child, but even the youngest of children seem relieved when a familiar bedtime routine begins in the evening, and they can relax for the night.

THE BIG BEDTIME BOOK OF BIBLE STORIES AND PRAYERS will help families make the most of the bedtime hour. With a selection of familiar Bible stories paired with contemporary stories, poems, prayers and activities, parents and children alike will find comfort in the reading, singing and praying they can share through the pages of this book.

As a parent, I find it important to give my children clues as to what stage of the night we are in. When we begin the routine of "pajamas on, read a story, have a drink, say a prayer, turn out the light" they are secure in the knowledge that their day is ending and they can relax in sleep through the night. Ending their day with a Bible story or prayer is a way that I, as a parent, can help my children feel secure in both my love and, more importantly, in God's love.

As you and your child read through this book together, you will probably find some favorite stories. Perhaps these stories will encourage you to tell some of your own. After all, story telling is one of the oldest forms of communication between generations, and one that can only help build the family bonds stronger from day to day.

My prayer for your family is for bedtimes that are blessed with love, peacefulness and the calm of a restful night.

In the Beginning

Once, a long time ago, the world was a dark and empty place. But God was there. God decided to change the world. First God said, "Let there be light!" And there was. Now there was morning and night on the first day. But God wasn't finished yet. God moved the waters to make room for the sky in the world. "I will call the ground land and the waters seas," God decided. "Now, let beautiful flowers and tall trees and green grass grow on the land."

God thought and thought about what to do next. Then God said, "Let there be lights in the sky to separate day and night and to give light to the earth." So God made two great lights for the world – the sun to shine like gold in the day and the moon to shine like silver at night. God also made the stars to twinkle and shine. Now there was sky and land and seas, and flowers and trees and grasses, and the sun and the moon and the stars.

Next God said, "The world needs living creatures of every kind to live in the water and fly through the air. I will make fish and whales to swim in the cool blue seas and birds and butterflies to float on the warm breeze." Do you think God was finished? No, not yet! The next day God said, "The world needs more living creatures." So God made animals of all kinds to walk on the land – lions and elephants and turtles and anteaters. God made all of the animals you know too – cows and dogs and cats and koala bears.

"This is good," God said. Then God decided to make a man. First God took dust from the dry land and molded the dust into a man. Then God breathed into the man and the man lived. God named the man Adam and took him to a special garden. "I have made this garden for you," God told Adam. "I know you will take care of it for me." God looked around at all that He had made and He was happy.

But Adam wasn't happy. Even with all of the animals and birds that lived in the garden, Adam was lonely. God took one of Adam's ribs and made a woman to live in God's world with Adam. Adam and Eve were happy in God's garden. They watered the flowers and trees and they played with the animals and birds. Adam and Eve loved each other and Adam and Eve loved God.

God saw everything in the world and knew that it was very good. Now He had finished. God blessed the seventh day of creation and made it a holy day of rest for every living thing. (*Retold from Genesis 1*)

A Look and See Day

Day, Night –
Sleep Tight!

SUN

MOON –

STARLIGHT,

DAY

NIGHT –

SLEEP TIGHT!

"I want to, I want to, I want to!" Jeff said in a loud voice. (Some people might have said it was Jeff's yelling voice, but he didn't think so.) "I want to play outside!"

"But Jeff," his mom said gently, "it's raining cats and dogs outside!"

Jeff's mom was right. It seemed that it had been raining cats and dogs and elephants and giraffes for days and days. And Jeff and his mom and everyone in their family was getting tired of being cooped up inside the house. It would have been nice to go outside to play and escape the four walls of the house for a while, but ...

"That's it," thought Jeff's mom, "why shouldn't we go for a rainy day walk?"

"Jeff," Mom said, "why don't you put on your boots and raincoat? Who says we have to stay inside for another day? We can go outside and have a rainy day walk!"

Jeff jumped off his chair. "Really, Mom? Will you really let me go outside in the rain? Will you come with me?"

Mom's only answer was to bend down to put on her own boots and slip into her raincoat.

It was hard not to splash in the puddles that had collected all around. Jeff didn't try very hard to miss the puddles in his path, but Mom was a little more careful.

SPLASH, SPLASH, SPLASH!

"Mom, this is fun. Thanks for letting us come outside to play!" Jeff said happily as he splashed along the street. "Look, Mom, there's a rainbow in the street. How did that happen?"

Mom looked down near her feet. There was a rainbow in the street. "That's an oil rainbow, Jeff," Mom replied. "Oil from the cars that drive here is left in a thin layer on the street. When the roadway is dry, you can't see the oil, but when the rain starts, it makes puddles that catch the rain. When the rain mixes up with the oil, it makes the rainbows that you see."

As they splashed on, Jeff saw more and more things that looked different in the rain than they did on a dry day. Or maybe it was that Jeff had been inside his house for so many days that he was looking and seeing things in a new way.

After they had walked to the park and back, Mom said, "Jeff, I think it's time to go home. We need to get ready to make dinner. Maybe we could have a cup of hot cocoa when we get back, to warm us up inside and out."

"Well, all right," Jeff said with a hesitating voice, "but it sure will be hard to go back inside. I don't think the rain will ever stop!"

"Maybe not tonight," Mom agreed, "but it has to stop sometime. Anyway, we've had a great walk in the rain. Just remember all of the things that we saw today that were like new."

"You're right, Mom! And I have a great idea. I'm going to call this our 'look and see' day because we looked and looked at things to see them in a new way. I'm going to get out my watercolors and paint a picture of everything that we saw on our walk today!"

And that is just what he did.

The Zoo Boat

Once, a long time ago, there lived a man named Noah. Noah was a good man, and God was happy with the way Noah and his family lived. They took care of the things that God had given them, and they remembered to thank God for caring for them. But there were other people in the world who did not make God happy.

One day God said to Noah, "I want you to build an ark. It should be big enough to hold you and your family and two of every living thing on the earth. When you have finished the ark, I am going to send a flood to destroy the earth." Because Noah loved God, he did as God said.

After the ark was finished, Noah and his family took two of each living thing into the ark. When everything was ready, God shut the door. Then the rain began to fall. It rained hard for 40 days and 40 nights, until a flood covered the entire earth. But Noah and his family and all of the animals were safe inside the ark.

Soon God sent a warm wind over the earth to dry up all of the water. Noah sent a dove out of the ark to see if there was any dry land yet. But the dove came back to Noah. "That's all right," Noah said to the dove. "Soon God will let us see dry land again." One week later, Noah sent the dove out of the ark again, and this time the dove came back with an olive branch in its beak. One more week passed, then Noah sent the dove out of the ark for a third time. This time the dove found dry land and stayed in a tree top to make a nest.

MY RAINBOW WORLD

God made me part of a rainbow world!

There are blue skies, white clouds,

and forests of green;

There are red and orange flowers,

and more to be seen!

People are part of my rainbow world, too;

God made them that way

From the very first day!

No matter where I look,

no matter what I do,

When I look the world over

I find that it's true:

The best part of God's rainbow

is just me and you!

Finally God said to Noah, "Now it is time to open the door of the ark. Bring your family and every living thing with you out into my clean, new world." When they came out of the ark, Noah and his family gave thanks to God for keeping them safe. "Look up in the sky," God said. "The rainbow you see in the clouds is my promise that never again will there be a flood that will cover the earth. Every time you see a rainbow, you can remember my promise." (*Retold from Genesis 6:9-9:17*)

Mr. Noah's Pet Shoppe

Mr. Noah had the best pet shop for miles around. The sign over the door read, "MR. NOAH'S PET SHOPPE", printed over a big striped rainbow. On one side of the rainbow there was a picture of a giraffe taking a bite out of the rainbow. And on the other side of the rainbow were pictures painted of some of the pets Mr. Noah kept in his shop – puppies and kittens and fish in a fishbowl and, of course, a parrot that could talk.

All of the children who lived in Mr. Noah's town loved to come and visit him and the animals he kept in his pet shop. Whenever their own pets at home were sick or not doing too well, children would come and ask Mr. Noah for his advice. And whenever Mr. Noah's pets in the shop were feeling blue, Mr. Noah would invite the children in to help cheer them up.

The mothers of the children who lived in Mr. Noah's town couldn't quite understand why Mr. Noah always seemed so happy after the children had been in his shop. "Why, your children are so helpful and pleasant when they visit MR. NOAH'S PET SHOPPE," he would tell the mothers. "They always seem to know just what to do to help cheer up an animal that is sad, and they help feed and water all of the animals without even being asked!"

Of course, the mothers couldn't quite understand this, because it seemed that at home they always had to ask their children to help over and over and over again. What was Mr. Noah's secret for getting the children to help so cheerfully? One mother decided to try to find out.

It was easy for this mother to find a reason to be in the pet shop. After all, she was out of goldfish food and needed to buy some right away. But when the school bus dropped the children off at the corner, she needed to find a place to hide. She didn't want the children to see her spying on them in MR. NOAH'S PET SHOPPE, so as the shop doorbell tinkled the mother ducked behind the shelf.

"Squawk, squawk! Hello, hello!" shouted Hester the parrot. "Cracker, cracker, cracker!" she continued. The children laughed at Hester on her perch, then gave her the crackers she was so greedy for. "Here you are," they said, "time for your crackers, Hester. And time to clean your cage!"

Now the mother in hiding could hardly believe this! The children noticed that it was time to clean Hester's cage without being reminded? How did Mr. Noah do it?

Then the mother noticed the children gather around a chalkboard in the back of the pet shop. Mr. Noah was there, too, with a snack for the children to eat as they talked and giggled about their day. Even though the sounds of children talking and animals chirping, mewing, barking and splashing were noisy, the mother could still hear the questions that Mr. Noah was asking the children: "How was school today? Did you know, today I learned that a tarantula sheds it skin every two years, and it even crawls all the way out of its eight legs! Did you have a good recess, even when it began to rain? Whose turn is it to take Muggs for a walk today?" And the questions and information that Mr. Noah shared with the children went on and on. The mother also noticed that Mr. Noah took time to listen carefully to what each child said, and made sure that everyone got a turn to do the favorite jobs in the pet shop that were listed on the chalkboard. All of the children worked with a partner, and Mr. Noah had the children who did the job last time teach the newest children what to do.

"Hmmm," the mother thought as she watched and listened. "Mr. Noah keeps order in his pet shop by letting everyone share in the responsibility. And he teaches them how to help and respect each other by the way that he helps and respects each one of them! Maybe the mothers and fathers of the children in this town could learn something about how to treat our children from Mr. Noah."

A RAINBOW ON YOUR WINDOWSILL

• Fill bottles with colored water to make your own rainbow on a windowsill!

• First, find six or seven clear glass or plastic bottles that will fit on your windowsill.

• Put three or four drops of food coloring in the bottom of each bottle, then fill the bottles with water. Make your colored water the colors of a rainbow – yellow, red, purple, blue and green. You can mix drops of food coloring together, if you like, to make even more colors.

• Line up the bottles in a window and watch for a rainbow to shine through on a rainy day.

The Most Beautiful Coat

Once, a long time ago, there lived a father who had twelve sons. Of all of his twelve sons, this father loved his son Joseph more than all the others. He gave all of his sons new coats to wear, but Joseph's was the most beautiful coat made of all the colors of the rainbow.

When Joseph's brothers saw his beautiful coat, they were jealous. Every brother wished that he could have a coat like Joseph's coat!

"Joseph is treated better than we are," the brothers grumbled to each other. "It's not fair!"

SLEEPYHEAD

- Now it's time to go to bed!
(*raise arms over head and yawn as if sleepy*)
- Time to rest your sleepy head.
(*rest head on hands with eyes closed*)
- One more drink, a story, all right,
(*pretend to be turning the pages of a book*)
- A hug, a prayer, turn out the light
(*cross arms over chest to hug self*)
- Now it's time to say goodnight.
(*fold hands in prayer*)
- So close your eyes, you sleepyhead,
(*close eyes and rest head on hands in sleep*)
While angels rest beside your bed.

One day when the brothers were out working in the fields, their father sent Joseph to find them. The brothers saw Joseph's coat with the colors of the rainbow from far away.

"Look, Joseph is coming!" they said. "Let's steal his colorful coat and throw him down the well."

One of the brothers wanted just to scare Joseph by throwing him down the well and then setting him free, but the other brothers sold Joseph to men traveling to Egypt. Then the brothers went home and told their father that a wild animal had killed Joseph.

When Joseph was in Egypt he worked very hard. But God always took care of him. When Joseph's brothers came to Egypt to buy food, Joseph forgave them for what they had done long ago.

"I am not angry!" Joseph told his brothers. "I will help you, just as God has always helped me."
(*Retold from Genesis 37: 39-49*)

The Missing Piece

Josie was tired. But not that tired! Even though Mom and Dad had told her to get her pajamas on RIGHT AWAY, she knew they weren't really angry. Josie knew that every night at bedtime there was always time for a story, a drink, a hug and maybe a song. And of course, there was always time to pray a bedtime prayer together, thanking God for all of the good things that had happened that day.

"All right, Josie-Jo," Dad said as he opened the bedroom door. "Are you ready for bed?"

"Just about, Dad," Josie mumbled as she finished slipping her arms into her pajamas.

"OK, now I'm ready for a story!" she said.

"I know," said Mom as she sat down on the bed next to Dad and Josie. "How about the story of Goldilocks, or one of our favorite Bible stories about Jesus and his friends?"

As Mom spread the faded quilt over Josie and tucked it in around her, Josie knew what story she wanted to hear tonight.

"Tell me about the missing piece," Josie begged, "the missing piece of my quilt!" Even though Josie had heard this story almost a million times before, she wanted to hear it again tonight. After all, it was one of her favorite stories, especially because it was about her Grandma Rosa and her mom and herself.

"Oh, good," Mom said. "That's one of my favorite stories too."

And so she began ...

Once upon a time there was a little girl. Now this little girl lived a long time ago. Her name was Rosa.

Rosa had brown hair that she wore in long braids, and bright blue eyes, and she liked playing jump rope and dolls and climbing trees. But most of all, Rosa liked to help her mother cut and sew patches together to make quilts.

Rosa's mother was a seamstress and she made beautiful clothes and quilts. And Rosa learned to sew doll's clothes and make doll's quilts from her mother too. One day Rosa's mother told her that it was time to start sewing a real quilt – a big one that Rosa could use on her own bed.

At first, Rosa had fun cutting and sewing and sewing and cutting. But a big quilt was a lot more work than a quilt for a doll's bed!

Time passed and Rosa grew up and got married and had a baby of her own. One day, she pulled the quilt out of the corner of the closet and she started working on it again for her own baby.

But babies take a lot of time! Even though she liked cutting and sewing and sewing and cutting, Rosa didn't have time to finish the quilt so she left one corner of it unfinished.

Rosa thought, "If I tuck this quilt into the corner of the bed just right, no one will see the missing piece."

"Besides," Rosa said to herself, "a quilt is made with scraps of fabric and thread, all stitched together with love. As long as I leave a missing piece on this quilt, there will always be room for someone else to add their own stitches of love to finish it!"

And that is just what Rosa did! And do you know, to this very day, that quilt still has a missing piece – if you look closely in the corner of your own bed, you might see it!

A RAINBOW PILLOWCASE

● Take a plain pillowcase. Use fabric paints to paint rainbow stripes, circles and other shapes on the cloth.

● When the paint dries, put a pillow inside and dream about rainbows while you sleep!

Rules to Live By

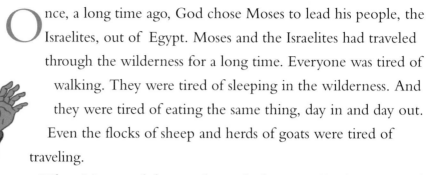

Once, a long time ago, God chose Moses to lead his people, the Israelites, out of Egypt. Moses and the Israelites had traveled through the wilderness for a long time. Everyone was tired of walking. They were tired of sleeping in the wilderness. And they were tired of eating the same thing, day in and day out. Even the flocks of sheep and herds of goats were tired of traveling.

When Moses and the people reached Mount Sinai, Moses said, "Let us stop here. You can get water for your animals here, and put up your tents for the night. When you build your fires for the night, you can bake bread for your evening meal. Then you can rest."

The Israelites were glad that Moses let them stop and rest on Mount Sinai. Moses was glad they had stopped, too. Just like everyone else, Moses was tired. But even though Moses was tired, he wanted to take time to talk to God. Long before this, God had convinced Moses that he was the one to lead the people out of Egypt, to the land that God promised them. But sometimes Moses wasn't so sure. After he had rested for a bit, Moses went up on the mountaintop to talk to God.

God said, "Tell my people that if they obey God they will be a holy nation and my special people." So Moses told the people what God had said. Then Moses went back up on the mountain, and God Himself spoke to the people. When He spoke, the people saw a thick cloud at the top of the mountain, and heard thunder crashing in the sky. The people saw lightning flash all around the mountain, and many were afraid. Moses climbed all the way to the top of the mountain to listen to God's words. God said, "I am the Lord your God who brought you out of the house of Egypt. You shall not have any other gods than me. You shall not use my name in a wrong way. Remember my holy day. You shall not kill, or steal or tell lies. You shall not want something that does not belong to you."

When Moses came back down the mountain, he told the people what God had said. "These are the rules that God has given us to live by. If we follow these rules, we will be living our lives the way that God wants us to." (*Retold from Exodus 20:2*)

N-O Spells NO!

Some days it seemed like Megan's little sister, Jenny, only knew one word – "No." It got a little tiring to hear that one word over and over and over. "Jenny, will you pick up your toys?" "No," would come the reply.

"Jenny, will you feed the dog a bone?" "No," she would answer.

"Jenny, it is time to go to sleep now!" "No!" she would shout.

Everyone wondered, "Do you think Megan's little sister will ever learn to say anything besides 'NO'?"

Even though Megan's mom and dad tried to tell her little sister how important it was for her to listen to them and to do what they told her to do, Megan's little sister still didn't follow directions. She just said "No".

One day, Megan's little sister was following Megan all around the house. Now it was Megan's turn to show her little sister what "NO" meant!

"Megan, can I play with you?" Megan's little sister asked.

"No," was Megan's reply.

"Well, can I use your tape player and new tape and book to listen to?" she asked Megan.

Can you guess what Megan's answer was this time? You're right. Megan just said "No". In fact, Megan just said "No" to every single thing that her little sister asked her. ("Hmmm," thought Megan, "this is kind of fun!") But it wasn't fun for long.

When Megan's mom and dad came home, they realized what was going on. In fact, they had thought about saying "No" to Megan's little sister before, too! But still, they knew that even though it was important to know how to say "No", it was also important to know how to say "Yes".

"Time for a family meeting!" Megan's mom and dad called to the two girls. "We have some important things to talk about tonight."

A BEDTIME PRAYER

Dear Lord,

Thank you, Lord, for another day of living in the world that you have made. Help me to remember to take care of your world, and of all the people and animals that share it with me. Help me to remember, too, Lord, that it is important to have rules to follow, and that you have said "Yes" to loving me, just the way I am.

AMEN

When Megan and Jenny came to the dinner table, they were both out of sorts. Megan was tired of saying "No" all the time, and her little sister was beginning to see why everyone got so mad at her when she said "No" all the time.

"Now," said Dad, "we need to review our family rules to make sure that everything is running smoothly."

"When we ask someone to do something," Mom said, "we expect their help. We all live in this family together and we all have important jobs to do. When someone always says 'No' it makes us feel pretty bad. Doesn't that person know that rules are rules? We have to have rules for lots of reasons, but one of the main reasons we have rules is for safety. What would happen if we said, 'Don't play in the street' and you played in the street anyway? You could get hit by a car or a bus."

Then Dad added, "Do you remember the story about Moses and the Israelites traveling in the wilderness? They had been traveling for a long time, and they were sick and tired of it! They weren't very grateful to God, and then God gave them a list of rules to follow! Those rules were the Ten Commandments, and they helped the Israelites live the way that God intended people to live. We need to remember those Ten Commandments today too. But we also need to remember not to always say 'No' when someone asks us to do something. We need to remember that sometimes 'Yes' is the most important word that we can say."

Megan's little sister finally looked up from her dinner. "I'm sorry that I always say 'No' all of the time. Can you help me learn to say 'Yes' more?"

"YES!" Megan, and her mom and her dad shouted all together. And then they all began to laugh.

A Boy and a Giant

Once, a long time ago, there lived a shepherd boy named David. David was happy when he was being a shepherd and taking care of his sheep. Sometimes, when David was taking care of his sheep, he played music for them on his harp. David even liked to write words and music to tell God what he was thinking. Some of David's words and music are the Psalms that you can read in the Bible today.

David loved God very much, and God had a special plan in mind for David.

One time, there was a giant who was over nine feet tall! All of the king's soldiers were afraid of the giant, whose name was Goliath. Goliath wore a metal helmet and metal armor all over to protect him from the soldiers' arrows. Goliath wanted to fight the king's army because he was sure that he would win.

When David the shepherd boy heard that everyone in the king's army was afraid to fight Goliath, he thought to himself, "I am not afraid of Goliath! I protect my sheep all night and all day from the wolves that want them. I protect my sheep from falling down steep cliffs and getting stuck in the stickery bushes, I will take my slingshot and my stones and I will go and fight Goliath, the giant."

When Goliath saw David, the little shepherd boy, he laughed. "Who do you think you are, little shepherd boy? Do you really think that you can fight a giant like me? Ha!" But David answered, "You have metal armor and a sword, but I have God to protect me!" Then, as Goliath came forward with his sword to fight, David reached for his stones and his slingshot.

Ping! With one small stone, David hit Goliath right in the middle of his forehead. Goliath fell to the ground and died. Even though David was a small shepherd boy, with God to protect him, he fought Goliath and won. (*Retold from 1 Samuel: 16-17*)

> ## I CAN BE ANYTHING
>
> • I can play the piano
> (*move fingers as if playing the keys*)
> • I can run in place (*run in place*)
> • I can smile or frown (*smile, then frown*)
> in the middle of my face (*point to face*)
> • I can count to ten (*hold up fingers, one by one to show ten*)
> • I can sing A-B-C
> • I can be anything
> that I want to be (*motion different kinds of things, like rocking a baby or raising arm to hammer something*)
> • I like being me (*point to self*)
> and I just have to say
> that I'm really glad (*smile on face*)
> God made me this way! (*point up overhead, then hug self*)

23

Too Many Pockets

"Too many pockets! Too many pockets!" Mom mumbled to herself as she got everything ready to take to the laundry. "Seth has too many pockets with ... oooh!"

A frog? Was that a frog that just jumped out of Seth's pocket? Well, this was too much for Mom.

"Seth! Come here right now!" Mom yelled down the hall. Seth came right away. He knew Mom's "don't-fool-around-come-here-right-away-no-matter-what-you-are-doing-this-instant" voice.

"Nuts!" Seth thought. "She's probably doing the laundry and I forgot to clean out my pockets."

As Seth came around the corner, a frog jumped right in front of him. "Oops," Seth mumbled. "Sorry, Mom. I guess I forgot to empty my pockets."

"Young man," Seth's Mom began, "You have done more than forgotten to empty your pockets. You have entirely too many pockets and too many things inside your pockets! Why do you keep all of these things inside your pockets anyway?"

"Ah, Mom," Seth answered. "I never know when I'm going to need something that is in my pocket. Remember the time I was invited to Betta's birthday party, and her Mom forgot to bring candles for the cake? And I had some in one of my pockets. And then, I had bandaids in my pocket the day you cut your finger when we were picking blackberries, and ..."

"All right, all right," Mom interrupted. "I guess I can understand Band-Aids and candles and things like that. But a frog? And what about the time there was a pumpkin seed growing out of the dirt in one of your pockets? And the string that kept getting caught in the washing machine? That string was part of one of your pocket collections that just kept growing and growing and growing. When is it ever going to stop?"

Seth knew his mom was right. But he had tried all kinds of ways of making his collection smaller. He had used a backpack instead of pockets. That didn't work because all of the little things kept getting lost.

Then he had tried cleaning out his pockets every day, but it took so long to do that. And then sometimes he threw something away one day and discovered on the next day that he still needed it.

Sometimes Seth lost things in his own pockets and didn't know what he had at all. There was the school note about last year's Christmas concert. A birthday card he forgot to give to his friend, Ned, two years ago. The seeds he forgot to take to school for the seed experiment. Two pennies he found in

an old drawer and wanted to check to see how valuable they were. One smashed Nut Goody bar and three gum wrappers. His favorite yo-yo. And his slingshot.

All of Seth's other friends had the newest water guns and laser beamers. But Seth liked sticking with his trusty slingshot, just like the one David the shepherd boy had used. After all, David had used his slingshot to kill the giant, Goliath, many long years ago. Who knew when Seth might need his slingshot to help someone someday?

On his way to school the next day, Seth saw Mrs. Petterson's new kitten stuck up in a tree. That wasn't too big a problem, but guess what was stuck in the branches, right near the kitten? A bee's nest!

As Mrs. Petterson stood below the tree calling to her kitten, Seth looked the situation over. Then he said to Mrs. Petterson, "I think I can help get your kitten out of the tree with my slingshot!"

"How can you do that?" Mrs. Petterson asked, "If you hit my kitten with the slingshot, or even if you hit the bee's nest, that won't help at all!"

But Seth had a plan. With his slingshot and a small pebble that was lying on the ground, Seth took careful aim. If he had the pebble just right, it would hit the nest and knock it off the branch to the branch below. Luckily for Seth, he had already climbed that tree earlier in the week and had seen that no bees were living in the bee's nest. With just a light tap of the pebble, the nest and the tree branch would shake and the kitten would want to come down to be safe! As Mrs. Petterson stood underneath the tree branch, Seth's aim hit the mark. Ping! The tree branches began to shake, the empty bee's nest fell down, and the little kitten jumped safely into Mrs. Petterson's arms. "Oh, thank you, Seth," Mrs. Petterson's whole face beamed as she thanked him.

"It was nothing," Seth said as he walked home whistling. "I can't wait to tell Mom about how important my pockets are!"

The Lion's Roar

Once, a long time ago, there lived a man named Daniel. Daniel lived in a land called Babylon. Daniel was a good man who loved God very much. No matter what happened, Daniel was faithful to God. When other people forgot about God, Daniel remembered. He remembered to pray and thank God every day.

The king of Babylon, a man named Darius, needed wise people to help him rule his country. One of the wise people he chose to help him was Daniel, but the other wise people were jealous of Daniel. They knew that the king listened carefully to Daniel and followed his advice. They worried that one day the king would choose Daniel to be the new ruler, so they thought of a way to trick the king and get rid of Daniel.

One day the officials came to the king and said, "Oh, King – you are so wise! We think that because you are so important, we should have a new law. We think that anyone who prays to someone other than you shall be thrown into a den of lions." King Darius thought this was a good idea, and it became law. Now the sneaky officials were sure that they could get rid of Daniel. They hurried to Daniel's house at noon, because they knew they would catch him praying to God. After they saw Daniel praying to God, the officials hurried back to tell the king.

The king was very sad when he heard about Daniel. But a law was a law. That night Daniel was thrown into a den of hungry lions. Just before the door was closed, the king said, "Daniel, I am sorry! May the God you love and serve save you!" That night, while Daniel was in the den of lions, the king couldn't eat or sleep because he was too worried about his friend Daniel.

Early the next morning, King Darius hurried to the den of lions. Before the guards could even open the door, the king was calling to Daniel, "Daniel, Daniel – can you hear me? Has your God saved you from the hungry lions?"

When the guard opened the door, Daniel walked out of the den. Daniel said, "You are powerful, King Darius, but my God is more powerful. He sent an angel to shut the mouths of the hungry lions. Surely you must know that even as I am faithful to my God, I am faithful to you."

King Darius was glad that God had saved his wise friend, Daniel. And Daniel served both God and the king for many, many years after this story was told. (*Retold from Daniel 6*)

The Lion Who Snored

Once, on a toy shelf in the room of some children, there lived a lion. Now, this was not your ordinary lion. Oh no! This lion, who thought he was the best and bravest of all of the stuffed animals on the toy shelf, this particular lion, had a problem. This lion – SNORED!

Every night, all of the other stuffed animals hardly got any sleep at all.

It seemed as if these other animals had tried everything. They had told the lion that he snored and do you know what he said?

"No, that couldn't be me! I hear someone else snoring all night long and it keeps me awake!" the lion argued.

So telling the lion about his snoring problem didn't help.

Then the other animals tried going to sleep first, so that they would already be asleep when the lion first began snoring. Do you think that worked?

No, it didn't! After all, some of the best fun of the day was after the children went to sleep, and the stuffed animals on the shelf didn't want to miss it.

They tried earplugs and warm milk. Didn't work. They hid their heads under pillows to see if that would help, but it didn't. They tried tickling the lion's toes with a feather from the stuffed parrot when he started snoring, just to see if they could make him stop. But that didn't work either.

They had just about given up hope, when one day the children's mother came into their room to clean it. "Look at all these toys," she said as she shook her head. "Something has to be done about all of this. I think it's time to put some of the toys away. I'll just need to go get a box."

After she left, the animals looked at each other in horror. What did she mean? Where was she taking them? Then, they wondered, "Who will she take to put away?"

When the mother returned, she hummed to herself as she took animals and toys off the shelf. By the time the mother was finished packing the box, the shelf was clean and dusted,

MY TEN FINGERS

I have ten fingers, you do too.
Here's what my ten fingers do:
- My fingers can do lots of things like counting bugs and tying strings; (*point to ground in counting motion, then pretend to tie a string into a bow*)
- They lace my shoes and button me. (*mime lacing up shoes and buttoning a coat*)
- They read a book and climb a tree. (*pretend to be reading and climbing, hand over hand, up into a tree*)
- My fingers help me wash my face and put my toys back in their place; (*motion to wash face, and to put toys back onto a shelf*)
- And at the end of every day, my fingers help my hands to pray. (*folding hands in prayer*)

A LION PILLOW

Take a round pillow and turn it into your own lion.
* Use felt or other fabric and cut ears to sew to one side of the pillow. Then cut out a mouth, nose, eyes and whiskers from fabric, or paint them on one side of the pillow to make the lion's face. If you cut fabric out for the face, you can glue or sew the pieces on.
* When you are done, you can put the lion pillow on your bed to sleep with every night. Maybe the pillow will remind you that just like when God protected Daniel from the lions, God will protect you.

and missing half of the animals that had once sat there.

Later that night, as the animals snuggled down to sleep, they yawned and stretched. And then, for the first time in a long time, they slept. The lion who snored had gone into storage!

Early the next morning, one toy bunny woke up, wriggled his nose and thought, "Morning! I feel great! I wonder why I slept so well?" The bunny looked around, then he noticed for the first time that the lion who snored wasn't there.

"Pssst! Pssst!" the bunny whispered to the other animals. "Where is the snoring lion? I can't see him anywhere! I slept all night. Did you?"

As the other animals woke up, they realized that they too had slept all night and hadn't even missed the snoring lion.

Right after the children left the room, they gathered around the bunny. "It was what we wanted, wasn't it?" grumbled a grouchy bear. "But I miss the lion," sniffed a kitten. "After all, he was my closest relative." "Well, I don't know about you," murmured the fuzzy caterpillar, "but I slept great!"

After they discussed life on the shelf without the lion, they all became quiet when the children came into the room. They heard the children talking, "Mom said she put all of the baby toys and animals away, but I think she took some of the wrong animals. I know my favorite lion is missing. I'm going to find him."

That night, after the children were sleeping, the bunny was the first to talk. "Hey lion! We hate to say this, but, well, we really missed you last night. We all feel much safer when you're here with us on the toy shelf."

"Well," the lion who snored began, "last night I thought how much I missed being with all of you, too. And I know that you don't like it when I snore, so I'd like to try to stop snoring, if you will help me. Then all of us can get a good night's sleep every night!"

So the animals took turns helping the lion wake up and turn over if he started to snore. But sometimes the animals just let the lion snore. They decided that his snoring was a reminder that he was still there, protecting them throughout the night.

A Fishy Tale

Once, a long time ago, God had a message for the people who lived in Nineveh. Who could God send to take the message to the people? God remembered Jonah. God said to Jonah, "Go to the city of Nineveh. The people who live there have not been living their lives the way that I want them to. Warn the people that unless they change the ways they are living, I will punish them."

Jonah thought about what God had told him. "I don't want to go to Nineveh," Jonah thought. "Why should I be God's messenger?" So Jonah ran away from God. He found a ship that was sailing far away from the city of Nineveh. At first, everything was fine on the ship. But then a storm came up. First, the wind began to blow like this - whoo! - whoo! Then the waves began to splash! Higher and higher, the waves splashed and crashed around the boat that Jonah was on, hiding from God.

"What is happening?" the sailors shouted over the splashing and crashing of the storm. As the waves rocked the ship to and fro, the sailors began to throw things overboard to help save their ship. The sailors were afraid! Finally the captain of the ship went looking for Jonah. He couldn't believe his eyes - Jonah was sleeping!

"How can you be sleeping in the middle of this storm?" the captain shouted as he shook Jonah to wake him up. "Wake up! Maybe if you pray to your God we will be saved." Then the sailors began to wonder who Jonah was. "We are wondering," the sailors said to Jonah, "if maybe this storm is your fault. We have never seen the waves so big or the wind so fierce as it is today."

"You are right," Jonah told the sailors. "It is my fault that we are in the middle of this storm. God asked me to be a messenger, but instead I am running away. If you throw me into the sea, the wind will die down and the waves will stop."

At first, the sailors were afraid to throw Jonah into the sea. But when they finally did, the wind stopped and it became calm on the surface of the sea. But under the sea, where Jonah was, God had sent a fish as big as a whale. The fish opened his mouth wide and swallowed Jonah!

MY HIDING PLACE

Sometimes I like to hide from everyone.

They call my name over and over, but they can't find me.

Sometimes I hide under my bed with my favorite bunny.

Sometimes I hide in the attic by the big gray trunk.

When they look for me, they don't think I might be hiding under the table.

Or under my favorite blanket.

On sunny days I like to hide between the sheets and

blankets drying on the clothesline.

I like to hide when I am sad or lonely.

And sometimes when I am really, really angry.

I like that it's quiet when I hide and I can think to myself.

Or sing a song that I want to sing.

Last summer we built a treehouse that I can hide in.

But sometimes I just like to climb a tree and hide in the branches.

I don't think I would like to hide in the bottom of a boat like Jonah did.

When I hide in any of my favorite places,

I know that God still knows where I am.

Jonah was inside the fish for three days and three nights. It was dark inside the fish and there was nothing for Jonah to do but to pray to God. "God," Jonah prayed, "I know that you always hear me when I pray. I'm sorry, God, that I didn't want to be your messenger! I'm sorry that I ran away from the city of Nineveh." Then God made the big fish spit Jonah out onto the beach.

God told Jonah again, "Go to Nineveh and give the people my message." So Jonah obeyed God. Jonah walked and walked and walked the many miles to the city of Nineveh. Jonah told the people what God had said, and the people believed what Jonah told them. They decided to change the ways that they were living and live the way God wanted them to.

Now Jonah got angry with God. "God," Jonah prayed, "why did you make me come here? What a waste of my time. Now the people of Nineveh have changed their ways and are living the way that you wanted them to live. Now you won't even punish them at all!" Jonah was so angry, he went outside the city walls and sat in the sun. Jonah kept hoping that God would change his mind and punish the people. But God didn't change his mind. Because the people of Nineveh had changed their ways, God didn't punish them. (*Retold from Jonah 1-4*)

My Goldfish Bowl

I have a goldfish bowl, do you?
It's round and full of rocks;
I wonder as fish flip and flop
if that is how they talk.
At splish-splash time in my goldfish
bowl
they twirl 'round and 'round;
They move so fast the water spins,
yet they don't make a sound.
I sometimes wonder when
fish sleep,
if they close their eyes or
not;
Or how they cool off on
a summer day
when it's nice and hot.

The goldfish in my goldfish bowl
can splash and dart and dive;
I'm glad God made my goldfish –
they're glad to be alive!

SHADOWS

● Have you ever made pictures
with your hands? It is easy to do when you
have a bright light shining on a wall, and
you use your hands to make the shadows.
● Try making hand shadows at night when
you are in bed. Use your night light and try
to make a fish, a duck, a camel or a cat.
What other animals can you make?

The Angels' Song

Once, a long time ago, baby Jesus was born. Mary and Joseph had heard the news that everyone had to travel to their hometown to be counted for the census. Mary and Joseph had to travel to Bethlehem. First, they got everything ready – food and water for them and for their donkey. They took soft blankets with them because Mary was going to have a baby, and they knew the baby could be born while they were in Bethlehem.

It was a long, tiring journey. When they got to Bethlehem, the city was very crowded. Joseph knew Mary was very tired. "I will find us a place to stay, Mary," Joseph told her.

Joseph knocked on many doors, but every inn was full. Finally, Joseph went to the last inn. "Please, innkeeper, we are very tired and my wife, Mary, will be having a baby soon. Do you have room for us for the night?" As the innkeeper shook his head, he noticed that Mary and the donkey looked very tired. So as Joseph turned away to go back to Mary, the innkeeper said, "Wait! I don't have room in the inn, but I do have a nice dry stable in the back. You can stay there if you like." Joseph thanked the innkeeper and led the donkey to the stable. That night, baby Jesus was born.

It was late at night when Jesus was born. Everyone in Bethlehem was asleep – everyone, except some shepherds who were watching their sheep. Suddenly, in the quiet darkness, a great light shone around the shepherds and their sheep. As the light got brighter and brighter, the shepherds were afraid and they hid their eyes. Then they heard the most beautiful song they had ever heard. It was angels singing!

The angels sang: "Glory to God in the highest, and peace on earth." As the shepherds peeked from behind their hands, one of the angels said, "Don't be afraid! God has sent us to tell you the good news. Tonight, God's son was born. You can find him in a manger in a stable in Bethlehem. The light of the brightest star will lead you to him."

"Let's go to see this baby who was born in a manger," the shepherds said to one another. They ran to Bethlehem, following the star that shone over the stable. There in the stable, lying in the manger, just as the angels' song had told them, was the baby Jesus. After the shepherds had seen the baby, they knew it was time to return to their sheep. On the way back, the shepherds stopped everyone they met and told them, "Listen! We have good news to share with you! Tonight, in Bethlehem, God's son was born!"
(Retold from Luke 2)

The Best Gift

Once, not long ago, a little girl was thinking about Christmas. She was thinking about all of the very good things about Christmas – the presents and the cookies and the beautiful Christmas tree. And she was thinking about her favorite things about Christmas – the stockings hung by the fireplace that she found filled with candy and toys on Christmas morning, and chocolate fudge, and hoping it would snow.

But she didn't even know about the real meaning of Christmas.

This little girl was a happy little girl – at least, most of the time. She knew that she was lucky to have a family that loved her, and a warm house to live in, and enough food to eat every day. She even had pets to love and a big backyard to play in with her friends.

One day, in the month before Christmas, a friend invited her to come to a party. The little girl loved parties so she decided to go. But as she soon found out, this wasn't an ordinary party.

This party was in a building where people lived who had no place else to go. Some of the people were old. Some were young. There were even whole families there! Some of the people who lived in the building were sick, but others just couldn't find a job.

As the little girl looked around, she didn't see all of the nice things she had in her own house. No one had their own room to sleep in. Even though the children's clothes looked clean, they weren't new. And there were hardly any toys to play with at all.

But one thing she did notice was that the people looked happy. They were talking and singing, and laughing together as they worked around their building. The little girl and her friend joined right in, helping some children build a block castle and then watching while another group of children used paper bags to practice a puppet show.

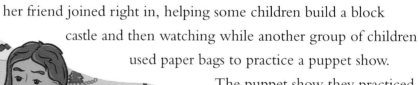

The puppet show they practiced was a Christmas story and they were practicing to perform for everyone in their building on Christmas Eve. The little girl noticed that the story they practiced wasn't about Santa Claus and his reindeer, or about opening presents under the Christmas tree. It wasn't a story about snow or eating cookies or a big Christmas feast.

No, this story was different – it was a story about a mother and a father and a donkey, traveling a long way. When they got to where they were going, there was no place for them to sleep. And the mother was going to have a baby soon. Thank goodness there was a kind innkeeper who let them sleep in his barn with the animals. And then, that night, the baby was born! The mother didn't have a special place to put the baby, so the father asked the animals if they would share their manger filled with hay with the baby. The animals nodded their heads, and then suddenly, a great light shone over the barn and there was singing! It was angels and they sang, "Glory to God in the highest for tonight His son Jesus is born!"

Right away, some shepherds came running to see the new baby. They had been watching their sheep on the hill and had seen the light and heard the singing. And then after they saw the new baby, they ran to tell other people. Even some wise, rich kings came to see the baby and left him gifts. One of the kings said something interesting.

"This gift isn't much to give to a king," the king said, "especially to the son of God. And you, little baby born in a manger, are the best gift that we could ever get from God."

When the puppet play was over, the little girl and her friend helped with the party. They served sandwiches and soup, and they shared cookies that they had brought for everyone in the building. Then together, everyone sang some Christmas songs. Funny how the songs also talked about the best gift that God had given to people – the gift of Jesus, His son.

When the little girl went home later that night, she thought about all of the things she loved most about Christmas. She still loved the Christmas tree and hoping it would snow and eating cookies. But now she had something else to love about Christmas – she knew the real story about how God had given His best gift to us. The real meaning was Jesus.

THE BABY IN A MANGER

We celebrate Jesus' birthday

A day when we recall

The baby in a manger

Who came to save us all.

A night when Mary and Joseph

In a manger filled with straw

Laid little baby Jesus

Only the animals saw.

Until …

The angels sang to shepherds

The shepherds ran to see

The baby in a manger

Wise Men on bended knee.

The baby in a manger

God's greatest gift, it's true,

The baby in a manger

Was born

for me

and you.

Brown Bread and Silver Fish

Once, a long time ago, Jesus was teaching people on a hillside. As Jesus looked out over the crowd of people, he thought, "It is getting close to lunchtime. I wonder if these people are getting hungry?"

Jesus said to the disciples, "These people must be getting hungry. Where can we buy them some bread to eat?" The disciples looked out at the crowd too. They saw how many people were sitting on the hillside listening to Jesus' teaching. "Jesus, there are so many people here. It would take so much money to buy bread for all of these people – we can't even count how many people there are to feed!"

Then Andrew, one of Jesus' disciples said, "I know there is a small boy here who has brought his lunch with him. He has five loaves of barley bread and two small silver fish. I know that he would share what he has, but that is not enough to feed all of these people!"

But Jesus believed that the five loaves of bread and two fish were enough. He said, "Tell all of the people to sit down. Then ask the boy with the bread and the fish to come to me." When the people sat down, there were more than five thousand people!

After Jesus talked to the boy, the boy gave Jesus his bread and fish. "Thank you," Jesus said to the boy. Then Jesus thanked God for the brown barley loaves and the silver fish. Jesus began to break the bread and fish into small pieces and the disciples gave it to the people. When everyone had eaten enough, Jesus asked the disciples to take baskets and collect any food that was left over.

As the people sitting on the hillside watched, Jesus' disciples collected twelve baskets of bread and fish. It was a miracle. But Jesus knew that when someone shares all they have, God blesses it even more. (*Retold from John 6:1-15*)

The Ants' Picnic

Have you ever been to a family picnic? It's lots of fun and everyone usually has lots to eat, plays fun games and enjoys seeing their relatives that they haven't seen for a long time.

Well, one warm summer day, it was time for the annual ant family picnic.

"Have you packed everything?" Grandmother Ant asked each ant that she saw. "It's almost time to leave!"

"Yes, Grandma," the little ant cousins all answered together. "We're just waiting until we hear the taxi coming!"

The mother and father ants hustled and bustled around the house, collecting last minute things like sunglasses and hats and blankets. The food had all been carefully prepared and was packed in hampers and baskets, ready and waiting by the door. Every ant knew that even though good food was packed in the baskets, some of the best food would be found when they finally reached the picnic grounds.

Soon the rumble of feet announced the coming of the taxi. It was time to go!

A BEDTIME SNACK

Nothing is quite as tasty as a warm piece of toast spread with butter, jam or honey right before bedtime! • Make a special bedtime snack by toasting your bread, then using your favorite cookie cutters to cut out the shapes you like.

• Maybe you will have heart shaped toast or maybe toast shaped like a bear.

• Once you have your toast shape cut out, spread it with your favorite topping. Mmmmmm!

• A cup of hot cocoa or milk will make a complete bedtime snack to enjoy.

What a great time the cousins had as they scurried to find their place in the taxi! Sometimes it was just a matter of luck to get a seat at all, but no one minded if they were in a tight spot because they had been looking forward to the picnic for such a long time.

"Aren't we in luck," Grandfather Ant announced to the group as the taxi rumbled out of the drive. "We couldn't have asked for more perfect weather! God is surely smiling on our family today."

Meanwhile, at the picnic grounds, the rest of the ant family was already gathering. Some of them lived fairly close to the picnic grounds, but others had traveled from a long way away. As they marched around in line, the ant family kept their eyes open

for the

perfect picnic spot.

Finally, they found the spot! Right near a large picnic table, with room to play games afterwards, and within a short walk of both the playground and the pond. This place had something for everyone. Just as the ants began laying out their picnic blankets and tablecloths, they heard the rumble of the taxi.

Little and big ants came running from every corner of the picnic grounds as they heard the taxi screech to a halt. Once the greetings had taken place, and children had run off to play tag and hide-and-seek, the ant parents settled down to talk about all that had happened to them since the last time they had met. And before they knew it, it was time to eat.

"Children, children," called the mother and father ants, "time to come and eat!"

After they had all gathered around the picnic table and joined hands, Grandfather Ant began the blessing:

"Dear God, We thank you for another year. For good weather and good friends in our family, and for the good food we are about to eat. Amen."

And now the real fun began, with the ants eating and laughing and chasing to find the best bits of food that they could eat. Of course, the ants enjoyed the food that they had brought with them on this picnic, but their special treats were the bits and crumbs that fell from the picnic table of the other people who were picnicking in the park as well!

On Jesus' Knee

Once, a long time ago, some people who loved Jesus were coming to hear him teach. Everywhere that Jesus went, people followed him to hear about how much God loved them. On this particular day, parents wanted to take their children with them to hear Jesus teach.

When the parents and their children came closer, the disciples said to themselves, "What are those parents thinking? Surely they aren't bringing their children to see Jesus – Jesus is much too busy to see children today!"

And the disciples tried to shoo the parents and children away. "Jesus is too busy, and besides," they said, "he is very, very tired."

But Jesus heard the disciples and he was angry with them. "That is not true," he told the disciples. "Come here," Jesus said to the children. "I am never too busy for you. God's kingdom belongs to children like you, and to people who believe in me like children do."

Then Jesus bent down to the children and talked with them. Jesus told the children about how much he loved them and about God's love for them. And he hugged them. "I love you," Jesus said to the children, "just the way you are." (*Retold from Mark 10:13-16*)

Jesus Loves Me
Jesus loves me, this I know,
for the Bible tells me so;
Little ones to him belong,
they are weak but he is strong.
Yes, Jesus loves me!
Yes, Jesus loves me!
Yes, Jesus loves me;
the Bible tells me so.

Kids Only

All the way to school, Jessica brooded about not being part of Kyle's club. Then all the way home, she brooded and worried about it some more. In fact, by the time Jessica got home from school, she was really feeling angry and left out. As she ran ahead of Kyle and his friends on the way home from the bus stop, Jessica made up a little rhyme in her head. It went like this:

Who cares? Not me!

I'll do something – Wait and see!

"Mom," Jessica said as she opened the door. "Can I have my own clubhouse?"

"Why do you want your own clubhouse? I thought when Dad helped Kyle and his friends build their clubhouse that the idea was that you could use it, too." Mom replied.

"Right! But they just won't let me in! They say they're too busy and too important for me, because I'm too little and I'm a girl. It's just not fair, Mom!" Jessica wailed.

"Hmmmm," Mom said thoughtfully. "I know that sometimes grown-ups can make kids feel left out, but I guess that other kids can do that too. Are you sure that there's no way to work it out so that you can all share the clubhouse?"

"Maybe," Jessica said. "But Mom, little kids like me aren't always pests, are we? And we have important things to do too, don't we?"

"Yes, Jessica," Mom said. "Remember the story about Jesus and his friends where the parents wanted to bring their children to see Jesus? Remember how the disciples told them that Jesus was too busy to spend time with little children? But what did Jesus say?"

Jessica remembered how Jesus told the disciples that he had time for children, because children really knew what it meant to love God. And he told them that people needed to and trust in him, just like children did, to belong to the kingdom of God.

After Jessica thought about Jesus and the children, she thought about Kyle and his friends. And about how angry she was and how she wanted to do something to show them that she was just as important as they were.

"I've got it, Mom!" Jessica smiled. "I'm going to offer to help Kyle and his friends by making a sign for the clubhouse. And I'm going to show them how the things that I have to say and do are just as important as the things they want to say and do. But most importantly, I'm going to be their friend, just like Jesus would want me to."

A Stormy Night

Once, a long time ago, Jesus had been teaching people for many days. He was tired, and knew that he needed to be alone to talk to God. So Jesus told his friends, the disciples, "Go into the boat and row across the lake to the other side. I will meet you there later, after I have talked with God."

The disciples rowed and floated along in the boat. They were tired, too. In fact, the gentle rocking of the boat put the disciples to sleep as they floated along.

Then, the wind began to blow harder. The waves around the boat got a little bigger, then a lot bigger. As the wind blew and the waves rocked the boat, the disciples woke up. They were afraid! "A storm is here!" they shouted to one another. "We are afraid! Where is Jesus?"

But Jesus knew that a storm was near. As the disciples looked out through the wind and waves, they saw someone walking on the water toward their boat. "How can this be?" they asked one another. "No one can walk on the water!" And they were afraid.

But Jesus called out to them, "Do not be afraid! It is Jesus, your friend. I knew that you were afraid in this storm and I have come to comfort you."

Now Peter, one of Jesus' special friends, called out, "Lord, let me come to walk on the water with you!" And Jesus reached out to Peter. "Come," he said. "Keep your eyes right on me." As Peter stepped out of the boat onto the water, he kept his eyes on Jesus. He could walk on the water too! Then, the wind blew a little harder. Peter looked down at his feet. He was afraid and he began to sink. "Help me, Jesus!" Peter cried.

Immediately Jesus reached out his hand and caught Peter. "Oh, Peter, why did you doubt? You knew that I would help you!"

Then Peter and Jesus climbed back into the boat. The wind died down. The waves became calm again. And they went on, rowing, to the other side of the lake. (*Retold from Matthew 14: 25-32*)

Splash!

It's my favorite time of night. Bathtime! First Mom makes sure that the water is just right. Not too hot and not too cold.

She asks me, "Do you want bubbles?" And I say "Yes!"

Mom lets me add the bubbles, then she tells me to go and get my pajamas.

When the bathtub is full of bubbles, it is time to climb in the tub. One toe at a time! I like to slide down into the bubbles and pretend I am hiding in the clouds. I wonder if God likes to hide in the clouds?

Sometimes I make a beard and mustache with the bubbles.

Sometimes I make a crown for the top of my head and pretend I am king of the clouds.

When the bubbles disappear, I take out my boats to play in the water. My boats swirl through the water and sound like this: putt-putt-putt.

If I slide back and forth, I can make waves for my boats in the bathtub. Mom doesn't like that, though. "Too much splashing!" she says.

When the water starts to get cool, I call Mom. "Time to get out," I say. Mom comes right away with a warm towel to dry me off.

When we've pulled out the plug, together we watch the water and bubbles swirl round and round, until they are all gone.

A Bright Night-Light

Sometimes, at night, it can seem awfully dark in your room! Make a special night-light to keep you company, and remind you that God is always watching over you.

Use a small night light that you already have or buy one at a store. Then find a pretty shell from the beach. (You can also buy a shell at a craft supply store.) A scallop shell is pretty, but there are other pretty shells as well.

Glue your shell to the outside edge of your night-light, so that when you plug it into the wall it will fit nicely. The light from the night-light will shine with a soft glow through the shell!

A Good Person

Once, a long time ago, Jesus told this story to the people.

There was a man who was traveling from his town to another. Suddenly, out from behind the rocks along the side of the road jumped robbers! One of the robbers grabbed the man and held him while the others took his money and his clothes. Then they beat the man up and left him lying in the ditch. As the sun rose in the sky, the man got hotter and hotter. He was sure that he was going to die.

Then, the man heard footsteps coming along the road. "Surely this person will stop to help me," thought the man. But when the man who was walking saw the hurt man lying in the ditch, he didn't stop to help. In fact, the man crossed over to the other side of the road and just kept walking.

After a time, the man lying in the ditch heard more footsteps. "This time," the man thought to himself, "this time, someone will see me and surely stop to help!" But the man who came down the road the second time didn't stop to help either. Would no one stop to help the man?

Then a Samaritan, who was a stranger from another country, came walking down the road. When he heard the man in the ditch moan in pain, the Samaritan stopped. He bent down to see the man who was in the ditch and he used a cloth and some oil to clean the man's wounds. Then he put bandages on the man and gave him a clean, cool drink of water. When the man was stronger, the Samaritan helped the man onto his donkey and took him to the closest inn. At the inn, the man from Samaria said to the innkeeper, "If I pay you, will you take care of this man until I come back for him?" The innkeeper agreed, and took care of the man.

After telling this story, Jesus asked the people, "Who do you think was the good person to the man who was hurt?" The people all agreed. "The man who stopped to help was the good person," they told Jesus. "Then go and do as the good person did," Jesus told the people. (*Retold from Luke 10:25-37*)

HELPING HANDS

* I have two helping hands
(*hold up both hands*)
* I use them each day
* I use them to work
(*use hands to imitate working actions*)
* I use them to play
(*pretend to bounce a ball*)
* I use them to clean
(*pretend to polish furniture*)
* I use them to sweep
(*pretend to sweep*)
* The only time I don't use them
* Is when I'm asleep!
(*rest head on hands as if asleep*)

I Can Help

Long ago, little girls could help carry water from the well.

I can help carry things too.

Long ago, little boys could help their fathers in the woodshop.

I can help my father in his woodshop too.

When Jesus was a little boy, children would take care of their brothers and sisters.

I help take care of my little brother too.

Children who lived in Bible times helped at mealtimes.

I help at mealtimes too.

Long ago, children helped their families just like I can help my family today!

MY HANDS

- Trace your handprints on to a piece of paper.
- Write your name and the words "I Can Help" at the top of the paper.
- Hang the paper where it will be a reminder to you of all the ways that you can help your family and God.

A THANK YOU PRAYER

Thank you, Lord, for every day that I have the chance to help someone.

Show me the ways that I can use my hands, my feet and my words to help

all of the people I know and love. And sometimes, if I'm not feeling very helpful,

show me how to be a good helper anyway.

AMEN

The Shepherd and the Sheep

Once, a long time ago, Jesus was teaching the people. Jesus loved to tell the people stories, and the people loved to listen to them. With the stories that he told, Jesus helped the people understand how much God loved and cared for them. When Jesus told stories, he told them in a way that people could understand. Sometimes he used examples about people who grew crops in the fields. Other times he told stories about shepherds who took care of their sheep. This is one story that Jesus told.

Once there was a shepherd who had 100 sheep. The shepherd took good care of his sheep. He made sure that the sheep had a chance to drink water from the clear cool stream. He made sure that the sheep had good green grass to nibble on. And at night, the shepherd made sure that he kept the sheep safe from wolves and other dangerous things.

One morning, the shepherd was counting his sheep to make sure that all one hundred of them were safe. One, two, three ... ninety-eight, ninety-nine ... But wait! One sheep was missing? How could that be?

The shepherd wanted to be sure so he counted again. One, two, three ... ninety-eight, ninety-nine. It was true! One sheep was missing.

Immediately the shepherd hurried to look for his lost sheep. The shepherd looked high and low. He looked under bushes and behind rocks. He checked by the river and next to the trees. Then, from behind some tall grass, the shepherd heard a sheep's voice saying, "Baa! Baa!" The shepherd hurried to find his lost sheep. He put the sheep on his shoulders and carried him home. And the shepherd told everyone he met that day how his sheep had been lost, but then found.

After Jesus told the people this story he said, "Did you know that God feels the same as the shepherd? When someone has forgotten to follow God, God is unhappy. But when that person returns to God, God celebrates in heaven." (*Retold from Luke 15:1-7*)

A Barnyard Evening

When evening comes in the barnyard, it begins very slowly. First, the sun sinks down and is swallowed by the hillside. Then, the air feels crisp and clean. The stars begin to twinkle, just a little, in the distance, and the moon is just a glimmer away.

The farmer feeds the cow a last handful of hay, and then checks all of the gates to make sure they are locked up tight. He leans down one more time to scratch the barn cat behind the ears, then whistles his way into the house for supper.

Now the only sound in the barnyard is the crunch, crunch, crunch as the cow chews her cud.

The barn cat licks her fur and cleans her whiskers just so. The chickens and the rooster fuss their feathers as they turn round and round to soften their nests.

BABIES ARE ...

Babies are little

but everyone loves them just the way they are.

Sometimes babies cry

but they laugh a lot too.

Babies make funny faces when they cry

but they make funny faces when they laugh too.

At first babies just drink milk

but then they start to eat lots of squishy things.

Babies like to play with things that make a noise

but they always like to taste everything they play with.

Sometimes babies sleep a lot

but other times they stay awake all night.

You and I were babies once,

but I'm glad that we're the age we are right now, aren't you?

The horse snorts. The sow sighs. The sheep in the stall shake their heads and the bells on their collars ring, ting-a-ling-a-ling, ting-a-ling. Outside, the wind whispers softly, "Goodnight to all, goodnight to all."

It is dark. The stars are twinkling brighter now, and the moon is not just a glimmer. The moon is bright and full. And the moon will keep watch over the barnyard throughout the evening, and into the night, until the sun comes up to begin a new day.

FLUFFY LAMB

Make your own fluffy lamb to hang on your bedpost at night.

• Take a white pom-pom (*you can buy these at a craft supply store*) or make one with white yarn. If you want to, you can bend two wire stems (*pipe cleaners*) and glue them to the pom-pom to make the legs.

• Cut a sheep face from felt and glue it to the front of the pom-pom. Tie a piece of ribbon at the top to hang the lamb from your bedpost. If you like, you can add a bell to the pom-pom where the lamb's neck is.

A Time to Help

Once, a long time ago, Peter and the other disciples traveled to many different cities to teach people about following Jesus. These were the days of the early church, right after Jesus had risen on the first Easter morning.

In one city there was a woman named Dorcas. Dorcas was a kind woman, with no family of her own. She was always helping other people and doing kind and good things for them.

While Peter was in her town, Dorcas became very sick and died. Everyone who knew her was sad. Two men that Dorcas had helped ran to find Peter. "Peter, Peter," they said, "please come quickly! Our good friend has become sick and died." Then they told Peter about all of the good and kind ways that Dorcas had helped other people.

When Peter got to Dorcas, he asked everyone to leave the room. Then he prayed to God, thanking God for Dorcas and the ways that she always helped other people. Then, Peter looked at Dorcas and said, "Dorcas, sit up!" And she opened her eyes and sat up! After a moment, Peter helped Dorcas stand up and come with him. Then everyone who had known Dorcas was glad that she was still alive. (*Retold from Acts 9:36-43*)

This Is ...

Do you know where wool comes from?

Do you know how sweaters are made?

Follow the words to this poem

and do the actions

and you will soon find out.

This is wool that grows on my back.

These are the shears that cut the wool that grows on my back.

This is the comb that combs out the snarls from the wool that grows on my back.

This is the way the spinning wheel spins as it spins the wool that grows on my back.

This is the yarn that is made from the wool that grows on my back.

These are the needles that knit the yarn that is made from the wool that grows on my back.

This is the sweater knitted from the yarn that is made from the wool that grows on my back.

NOW YOU KNOW HOW SWEATERS ARE MADE.

HELPER COUPONS

- Make coupons to give to people that you love to show the ways that you can help them.
- Maybe you can wash the dishes after dinner, or walk the dog, or clean your room.
- What other ways can you help?